THE DREADFUL NIGHT I RECALL

A DIFFICULTY WAY I WALK

JAGANNATH DAS

XpressPublishing
An imprint of Notion Press

Old No. 38, New No. 6
McNichols Road, Chetpet
Chennai - 600 031

First Published by Notion Press 2019
Copyright © JAGANNATH DAS 2019
All Rights Reserved.

ISBN 978-1-64650-487-9

Dedicated to:

Rabindranath Tagore,

Also known as Gurudev, Kabiguru and Biswakabi

Was a polymath, poet, musician, and an eminent artist

He reshaped Bengali literature and music as well as Indian art,

Author of the profoundly beautiful verse of Gitanjali, Gora, Jana Gana
Mana,   Amar Shonar Bangla etc so on and so forth

The first non-European to win the Noble prize in literature in 1913

Tagore's poetic songs are received as spiritual, mercurial and magnificent

He is referred as "the Bard of Bengal"

-Author

Contents

Foreword

PRABHAKAR MALLICK

STUDENT OF (MPC AUTONOMOUS COLLEGE, BARIPADA), MAYURBHANJ

Life is not just a Journey, but a path full of adventurous experiences and intense feelings. Another words life is a zigzag way sometimes it is found the tears and sometimes found the smiles and it is called a life, no things are permanent. Your birth and death occurs in a cyclic process, no self-will works and it is strange still now: how do people die and after the death where the chapel to reach his/her soul? Your birth time-period decreases wherever your death time period increases less by less on the entire life cycle of the life and it is everyone's blueprints on the palm of the hands. I have a platonic love towards Mr. Jagannath das. As a student, he writes this treasure in a poetry form when he faces some intractable problems in his life where no one may help to him. When I passed 10th exam 2013, I enter in college life but totally become an effected boy because of him, who always think about the values of life and dear and near who give a placid life. Simplicity he is to be an orthodox one not proudly said by myself. Once it so happened, sitting on a park, asked a simple question to him. This was a beautiful park with green creatures, Jagannath… I saw all and I also saw your happiness under your kind heart…. "But if this park is JURASSIC PARK, then what will you be doing": He replied "my body may move here in fear, but my soul will remain unchanged from enjoying the beauty of park"….I found only jokes on his comic remarks. But later I understood his short remarks show me about his personality. Truly speaking, he is a mad like man having past events he utters regularly. I always ask to forget that events: gone are the days: now begin a new life, but he needn't.

This book teaches us about reasons of love, faith in our dreams, to conquer from our both happiness and sadness, our life's decisions in end, your last destination. The emotional feelings as well as hateful things are found in our life. Moreover God always bless you to reach your successful journey.

Acknowledgements

Late Bankim Chandra Maharana:- educationist par excellence, poet, philosopher, national aware teacher etc.

Ajoy kumar panda:- a wordsmith, linguist, historian, commentator, poet, author of many books, his magnum opuses are Towards Eram Tragedy, The roaring Furnace, Lyrical pulse Beat of English Grammar etc.

Chandra sekhar Mantri:- Lect. In English, an architect of destiny of the students, a man of integrity in social life, believe in simple living and high thinking.

Pritam manna:- Adviser of Business and communication, give some hands to poor, well-wisher of many organization etc.

Sarbeswar Mishra:- the superintendent of head post office, bdk,756100

Antaryami Moharana:- a good benevolent person, work in social welfare organization.

TO WHOM I PAY MY RESPECT:

Mantri sir, Basanta sir, Sanjay sir, Senapati sir, Prasan sir, Hrushikesh sir, Muna sir, Dibya sir, Kedar sir, Praful sir, Ram sir, Pandit sir, Gobinda sir, Purna sir, padmini didi, Raja sir, Rabi sir, Nuru sir, Sudarshan sir, Manas sir etc.

MY OWN SOUL HIGHLIGHTS FOR:

For my father Mr. Pitambar Das, whom sagacious advice is responsible to look out my first poetry book.

My idol portrait:

Mr. Nilambar Das, EX-Headmaster from Ada High School, ada,Bls

MY DEEP AFFECTION TO MY BELOVED STUDENTS:

Kapish Raymohapatra, Debashis Panda, Asit ku. Behera, Nitya Prakash Das, Jay Krushana Prusty etc.

SPECIAL WISHES TO MY DEAR FRIENDS:

Narendra sahu, Satyaranjan Sethi, Shiba Sankar Bandha, Tapan Malik, Prabhakar Sethi, Pritam manna, Anjan panda, Ashok Bandha, Manoj kumar Panda, Shuvrajit Raymohapatra etc.

SPECIAL THANKS TO MY STAFFS:

Karunkar Gharai(SPM Sir), Rudra Babu, Ganesh Babu, Lambudhar Sir, Ramesh Sir, Gobinda Sir, Jagabandhu Sir, Surya Babu, Sanjay babu, Gauranga Babu, Rama Babu, Ashok Sir(IPPB), Shashi Sir, Smrti Babu ETC.

Prologue

The poetry book title "THE DREADFUL NIGHT I RECALL" is named in my heart. Life under the sun is transient crossing into a zigzag way of hurdles. In life's short way there is full of difficulties enclosed to you to lead a life of both tears and smiles where sometimes you have to walk on thorns, sometimes you have to walk on roses, and it is called a life. It is needless to say that the mirror is a perfect object for everyone's soul imagination means when you want to cry or smile, the mirror does the same. So without selfishness venom, it helps you to minimize your duties you do. Have you ever seen a night full of vampires, the fearful animals, the darkest area side on jungle at mid night? Somehow a person may arrive a forest, let it, later he is unable to find the perfect way to his destination. Now he is into the forest that he is confused what to do or what not to do in this crucial moment of panic stricken because soon evening approaches and within his eye's glimpse, the night falls more. He is running from side to side, he opens his mouth and asking for help, but all is going to come in vein. Think, he is the only person who describes or utter the fearful events in the darkest night but we aren't. Own difficulties must be described by a person who is on this way of life's journey but we aren't. "DREADFUL NIGHT" means a person feels the difficulties moments in life whenever he is walking under his social relationship with his dear and near. A person has encountered some sad problems in life and now he has lost all his confidence power, even confused how to live. This book holds this manner of feelings.

Writings of poet's first own pen:

This golden novel named: The dreadful night I recall" holds emotional as well as audacious feelings on the people's heart. However this book also indicates the difficulties in life and how to get rid of it. As a student, I write this treasure in a poetry form when I face some bad problems in my life where no one may help to me. Simplicity my first poem when I write, it is about my dear and venerable English teacher Mantri sir, who always supports to me because of him at first I write a poem: 'A portrait I recall' about a teacher's blessings to students. Some lines I describe:

'Your absence makes me so cool
 I walk I walk along the road,
When battle bell sounds a lot
 Y' r scenic portrait I recall'

Means a student always needs some sagacious advice in his life's battle field means when facing some difficulty situation in life whenever a teacher present or not that time. Moreover my all friends support me to publish this book. Then I write all emotional poems about the social life. I think my treasure novel in poetry form may steal the hearts of others and second edition may be published after your good wishes and happy feelings towards this treasury book.

A poet in 'The dreadful night I recall'

1. Battle field

Everyone knows that honor comes from fear but it is needless to say that sometimes for the honor, we feel fear in our heart and this is happening in the battle field. Moreover the poem shows this field is denoted only the signs of death and life and the warriors struggle tenaciously to achieve or resist their aims. The poet first describes the natural phenomena covered around the field and the line "it needs the body whom it wants" indicates the fearful sight around the field. Another line "when a bizarre situation happens no one think" means in the battle field there unusual fight happening without known before. The poem also tells that the more risks are found in night time than in day time. When the battle starts, some think they have no chance to return home where another some think that they may return to home. Keeping less-hopes when they shout as loud as they could, there the sounds disappear in the battle field at last. So battle field is a field of hopes and remorseless.

Battle field, battle field, battle field
Show signs of life and death......
Where always cover with black snow,
Remorseless story indicate the dread field.

It drinks the wine of red blood…
It needs the body whom it wants
There are the tussles prevent keeping silent,
When a bizarre situation happen no one think.
When the day retires from the field…
A reek origin there the devils come, look!
All the soldiers arouse from their slumber,
They run to destination keeping a dauntless heart.
Some feel they have no chance to return home,
But their faces have less hopes, may not happen it
So they sometimes shout as loud as they could,
But that sounds disappear in the battle field.

2. A portrait I recall

A teacher is the mirror in which students look their faces. By dint of a teacher's demeanor and nobleness, one can remember such teacher's duties throughout the life. The poem starts with the benevolent characters of a teacher. At first the poet calls the name of God for his teacher's good health and spirit. Then the poet thinks whether his teacher remembers or not about him, a poor student i.e. the poet but he always recalls the evergreen portrait of his teacher. The line "and I wait till the morning sun, shows me your idol" indicates a teacher is indispensable to mould a student's bright future and the love of a teacher and student is incredible. Time comes now the poet's life becomes sorrowful. The poet is unable to walk on his land of duties alones. Now the importance of a teacher is needed to show the right paths. The line "when battle bell sounds a lot, your scenic portrait I recall" means when the poet is in difficulties ways then he recalls the sensible and sagacious advices which is needed to lead him a prosperous life.

I hope in my heart I sure
You live in the best of your health and sprit
You remember y'r near and dear
The day I recall when I meet you.
Old memories are, come and go

THE DREADFUL NIGHT I RECALL

A portrait, an ever green portrait
Oft, I see into deep soul
And I feel- how pleasure it gives me!

I see a living God on your face
In y'r heart- I hear y'r kind words
My dream is only for you at night
And I wait till the morning sun
Shows me your idol……
Have an empty hearted,
In the desert, no sands of times
Now day is as dark as night
Aloneness makes me so fear..
Your absence makes me so cool
I walk I walk along the road,
When battle bell sounds a lot
Y'r scenic portrait I recall.

3. A weaver bird

The poem indicates two sorrowful events. First the poet feels despondent to think about the past and the second one is the poet's sorrows compare to a bird's journey in life. There the weaver bird don't break its strong determination whatever it happens but in other hands   the human beings are such animals who are unable to keep self-restraints. The poem begins that the poet remembers about the past sitting on a hillock. Pondering over the past when he is totally out of sense and eyes with tears, he discovers a weaver bird. A weaver bird's nest coiling with coir and threads hangs lower the palm tree. When the sky covers with black clouds and a flash of lightings when throbs our heart that time a weaver bird's heart isn't dreary inside the nest. The poet wants to say all that the weaver bird is, however, a dutiful bird. Again the poet focuses on its beak, is a war-beak. At last the poet changes his self moods and wants to know about the lives of bird may be fickleness or not, and how they feel both tears and smiles. The poet has no idea about it so he does not think more about the bird. Now once again he pondered over the past memories and it brings no cheers in his accursed life.

In a wintry day when I sit on a hillock
My sullen soul reminds about the past
When my heart is incarnated by a pity
I hear from the palm tree a bird croons.

Its nest as coil many coir and threads,
Lower the palm leaf it hangs in the sky
Tribal lands resound when it creaks,
The peasants are imbued by its amours.

A weaver bird without dreary and dismay,
When black clouds cover with thunder
Life's heaven and hell the bird sees its nest,
Alones he does its duty with its war- beak.

Their lives are a fickleness journey or not
How they feel both blithe and glum I think,
But I keep my memories that have gone…
And there are no signs to bring more cheer.

4. A walking traveler

A traveler walks. The poem "A walking traveler" means a person is waking to reach a destination where he has to go, he has to fulfill his duties. But in this poem this walking traveler loses all encouragements himself. He also loses his endeavor, boldness as well as self-assured. So as an empty vessel, he leads a life of predicaments. As his occupation is moving here and there i.e. walking traveler, he rambles in the desert showing his behavior like madness. The line "journey in the desert" indicates he is working hard but on the field of unsuccessful goals or events. Another line "a dry pond before my eyes" means all his enjoyable moments are depleted from the changing of time to time. Then the poet can understand the mistakes in life and some intricate questions arise on him. However the poet again says that before his eyes he sees a long distance stretched away, but he is unable to walk as his steps are wrongly footed on the thorns. The more distance you enter into the river, the more deep you feel so that in life's journey way the more distance you walk the more hurdles you find in life.

I rambled lonely as a walking traveler
Who wants to reach his end-less
journey in the desert.

An inconsolable child
No one trammels me as I always
Myself a mad and me a tippler
My open mouth always with
My lonely words....

Near the grassland I sit I think
About the past that I had
Tears come from my inward heart
Everywhere around me I feel all departed
And I gasp I gasp.....

A dry pond before my eyes
All is gone but never come
It a red letter day.
A cross line on my white paper
I feel all my gross mistakes,
An intricate question that arose on me,
What is life without the ultimate- happiness.

Outside the dearer and nearer
My heart as empty vessel
A long way before my eyes
But my steps are on the thorns else.

When you will begin to walk
At first you feel the river
With knee-deep water at coast
But no words you have to tell
How deeper than the river is:

5. Barefoot on the sands:

Life is transient and unpredictable. There also the things around us are not permanent. The nature also changes when requiring itself. Now what you have, later it is not found from you. The poem indicates that the poet is walking along the road and in thinkable mood. The poet thinks that the days which is gone, never come once more and all activities in life's journey i.e. scenic marbles for all, never come to all. The poet is walking and when he looks there the valley side a dry tree is seen out of all green trees. Later it changes or not only the nature know well. But the poet has no idea about it. The line " I listen the melodious songs at young" means the enjoyable moments with near and dear at the age of young. Another line "I drink with the world of its own accords" means the love of nature and what the society needs from you. Those things are slowly degradable with the changing of time. Now the poet finds nothing. There is a mirror but there is no near and dear to show in front of mirror and there is a ladder to lift but having no destination.

When I walk along the paths I want,
I utter some secrete talks arose on me
Gone are the days else never come
A scenic marble for all, never come to all.

When I keep a focus on the paths I walk
Around the world of me I found all lives
But my eyes find one out all treasures
Oh 'sadness a dry tree with its woes.

I walk with my bare-foot on the sands,
I see a tree cover the green-creature ago
I listen the melodious songs at young
I drink with the world of its own accords.

P.T.U

From the long distance when I come
My dear and near when they need me!
I hear some cries behind-the-scenes,

I feel some wobbly heads say not you go.
Day by day, months-years come and go,
There changes the nature when it needs
In my way all hurdles I cross when I face
I also drink the sweats of soul when I soil.
Now day is as dark as devils, have no signs
The Leaves turn into dry, no call of nature
There is a mirror, have no images of soul
I lift the paths of ladder but no destination.

6. Dream land

Dream land indicates a fantasy land. One can find alluring influences as well as vivacious feelings. Self prudent slowly decreases when you enter a dream land. It is a place of supreme bliss. The poet once slept on his bedroom. In the stilly night, eight hours a steady rain keeping his hovel its prey and the poet slumbered all night in a peaceful mind. Suddenly, according to him, he dreamt that of entering a land of fantasy. There the poet sees all different and marble things which he cannot watch before in his life. One's yeaning to enjoy the dream-land is in a tremendous degree. But the poet at last goes to a separate land by his boat, where he has to free from his own sins and sleeps forever.

When my own world caged me,
All things I need all-together.
All creatures dement me to live,
I enter a dream-land all around.
When I open the door of land,
It is hard to see in full of haze,
The sky with arch-rain bow,
A collage scenic sight I behold.
Birds with colorful wings,
All trees move in a way,
By sorcery they talk each with,
I take a shy in the breeze.

As a rover I sit on a swan,
It takes me a dream-brothel,
I look the shadows on ground,
Some bees return their Hives.

A river by side reflects along
in a direction of a milky-way.
Some hills on their crown-head
Adorn coy tiny-flowers I endear.
Near the drift-ice, a fairy land,
My wood-boat moves by oars,
towards the lounge for the soul,
need a nap free from foul sins.

7. Drollery man

This poem is in a jocundity mood. Drollery man means a man having no risks, no worries and no predicaments. His life always leads the dullness activities. Once a drollery man thinks how he eradicates the everyday's sorrows so that he could lead the prosperous lives forever. On account of this thinking, one day he walks the direction the sun rise. He rushes in between the fields he also enjoys the natural things. He thinks himself that all natural things want to free from all anxieties like him. Now the drollery feelings change in dullness. It so happens when he sees some fishes are into the fisherman's net, he stops that place and give a comic remark that if all natural things are coming with me for free from all wounds why those fishes aren't. When the drollery man removes the net, fishes are jumping hither and thither. One fish eagerly says to that man that you are the jovial-man as you escape me and my friends. Then the drollery man think if I m the jovial man, I will not need to walk to that direction for free from sorrows. So he comes back to his own house.

Everyday's sorrows all I have
In this golden morning of joyful events
the direction, for free from all wounds,
He faces the sun as a free-soul.
He walks in his eye-line
towards the fields of paddy-grains,
he touches the heads they stand!
the birds chirping, the twinkle-rays
all say him to turn a prettily life.

He thinks all follow the battle-cry,
the grasslands, the birds, the sun rays
the paths free from all anxieties,
so all with me..all with me....

Look! there are some fishes
Swayed in the fisher-man's net,
their blinking eyes regret, escape me!
I think if all is with me,
why not they come free from woes.
They give a frisky-jump,
When I remove ghost-net,
It begets you are the jovial man!
then passes in the deepest water.
So I return in a dubious thought,
no glooms full with life I feel.
Oft I think what the last fish utter,
I am the man of jovial.....so
No way to walk to my paths.

8. In the Farmer's way

The poem focuses on a farmer's social life. Since the beginning of civilization, we all depend upon him. Though they feed the entire humanity, their life conditions are far from satisfactory. This poem indicates a farmer's life is much dependent upon the forces of nature. A farmer and the nature's ebb are described in this poem. How fearful the natural climates are! Let's see: Once a farmer worked in the field. Suddenly he saw that the sky is covered with black clouds and around him it creates a long sigh storms with heavy winds and a repeated thunder. So what to do or what not to do before he decides, he runs across way to way. On his returning way, he saw the trees are rooted, cottage houses are destroyed, dust particles are covered everywhere, and his fellow-men's cry are reloaded repeatedly. This is the critical moment, according to poem, have no words on mouths of people. The line "in nature's key all fellow depart!" indirectly indicates that some people's death occur. Another line "when I cry out the direction I run" indicates the horror feelings because he ran and called the name of people loudly but no one could hear he lost everything that he had. At last he swooned and laid down on the bare-earth. Moreover the nature's severity come less by less and the torrent wind also moves slowly. Now the nature makes a wishful thinking to all after its cruelty effects. When he woke up, he saw a new world with him.

When I soil in my paddy-field

THE DREADFUL NIGHT I RECALL

In eye's glimpse, clouds are sailing
In the sky it begins a battle-voyage,
Soon it turns a day of black in its path.

The wind makes its queer sound
Old thirsty leaves roam to and fro,
Some rumors come from hell, run!
He gropes his way, full of dusts.
A thunder makes a dilemma-heart,
On the way he beholds nature's ebb,
In a heavy wind the rooted trees,
Cottage houses come fall, Run! Run!
No destination no paths for me,
In nature's key all fellow depart!
When I cry out the direction I run,
No sounds I hear the empty houses.
A torrent wind now moves slowly,
A wishful thinking the day after meet,
When I wake out of swoon all around
See a new world within me within me.

9. In love with a cottage girl

It is an incontestable fact that the feelings of love comes everyone's life and it stands supreme. It is a cementing force that binds two souls. It is said that for the love we can do something, the mountains may fall down but our natural love will remain unchanged till the death. You may love everything, everyone. But this poem holds a poet's internal feelings to a girl who is poor in her livings on a valley. The poet eagerly wants to know about her and her dwellings. So the poet faces to that green tea garden where aloneness she does her life's activities. She is nimble as well as placid according to poem. The poet feels curiosity about her aloneness duties on the valley. Time runs slowly and also it creates the natural feelings in poet's heart. When the poet reaches near the girl on the valley, he only looks some cottages attached inside the valley. So he calls the girl i.e., cottage girl. At last poet's excitements of knowing about the girl isn't successful because there the sun sets behind the mountain. She is punctual, so she goes back never talking my questions. But the poet thinks deeply that if she answers, it will be true or not, as she is a stranger. I may believe about her wrong answers as I meet at first knowing nothing before about her. Moreover time doesn't permit to poet to hear about her stranger lies or truths.

Her sweet and smiling face
Is always before me,
It seems as no difficulties

THE DREADFUL NIGHT I RECALL

in her placid life….
Standing up for an hour and hour
Her busy life I see from a distance
I feel on the entire valley-
She keeps awake herself alone.

On the green tea garden,
She looks as a queen bee.
With my keen eyes I
Look her look her.

Twinkling stars as her eyes…
Her heart is as gay as
A lark bird I feel…
But my heart and soul is
Incarcerated by a sudden tender pity,
Why, no one is seen…..

No one to help her on the entire valley,
No one to feel about her gracious heart,
And to see her graces,
Aloneness makes her so panic,
I have to feel she is my kin.

A soft wind began to blow,
And it creates a rustling sound
With my eagle-eyed I
Look her look her.

I move slowly nearby her,
My steps are on the steppe.
My questions arise behind her,
Hey goddess! Please say your name,
And say your dwellings....
Where your near and dear with
Make a funny role in lives.

Abruptly, she looks me,
In her goggle eyed it seems
A great thunder after a flash of lighting,
Some blossom smiles on her smile,
With my open mouth I
Look her look her.

Sun goes from east to west,
A bleak day soon ended, look!
"Someone waits for me" she says,
Then she runs as a queen bee
A small cottage house she faces.
I think some clinches she wants,
A stranger she may give a lie or a truth.
But with my open hand I have to back
And think let's come to another
Cheerful days come in my life.

10. Inside mother's knee

The poem reminds us old day memories. Here the poet takes us the place of our childhoods where funny activities going on. Moreover childhood is the vivacious moments of one's life. In this poem, poet's yeaning to go back on his childhood days, as a child all excitements stimulate upon his heart and soul. In another words it is the days of perfect freedom having no worries, no predicaments as well as no responsibilities. The poet has to say that mother's love and prosperity is like a valuable stone i.e. Gem, when a child falls in difficulties ways that time the gem glitters to solve the problems he/she faces. The poet once more says that call of mother is a holy name and the figure of mother is an ever green idol which is rarely found. The lines "your wraths when increase a lot, by spell my smile melts it down" indicates the importance of child's smile is a big weapon which defeats the sins of wraths. Another ways, you get a platonic love when listening the low voices and watching the blinking eyes of child. At last the poet when recall his mother's helpful duties he suffers in a sorrowful mood because the days with his mother never come once more and it is reality in life.

"When I move on the ground
Let me everything free from
My destination only towards you
When my days start in a hovel"

I am not an offal boy to you
In your knee, I keep to and fro
My blinking eyes may give you peace
My low voices may turn a heaven.

When I believe in creed
Without your knee, woe is me!
If your love and prosperity less to me.
Creed is cheerless to all, to all.
You make a mountain before me
When I do some deeds of dreary
Your wraths when increase a lot
By spell my smiles melt it down.
When I cross the difficulties
In life your holy name I utter…..
Let's worship an evergreen idol,
It never come a chance once more.

"I swear an oath not to swindle,
I never try to swerve the way alone
I cannot move the way without fear,
Ever they tease me in a dusky night"

"Where there embed the loves of gem,
In an obscure side I cry against the grim
There the gem glitters when it needs,
It brings some hopes to live... to walk..."
When I think about your helpful duties,
Its indefinite way almost not found...
When I am in my sullen-appearance
You suffer a swoon in y'r talks ....
Those days have never come yet
Some feelings I keep in my heart,
My mother is one among the earth
My mother is the last sign of me.

11. A Tormented soul!

Tormented soul means a person's heart is caused severe physical or mental suffering. A tormented soul is a soul that cannot break free. One's mental anguish seems when he is unsuccessful to do his life's duties. He also feels despondent after walking in an untrustworthy way. Later he slowly takes mental depression and his confidence power is seemed as graceless. The poem indicates that life is a slave and we are all under helpless victims. The poet is in an anger mood and asks to god why he is enclosed from all living things i.e. happiness and why in a throng fair he is so alone that no one have an eye on him. The lines "from mountain to hillock I run I run, fall on the knee I cry to free the flaws" indicates that the poet already knows his gross mistakes in life and he wants to free the flaws i.e. mistakes anyway. Another line "in my whole life leads a bond man" shows one's deadness feelings about life and he has no way to walk in life's journey. At last the poet wants the chapel to sleep in peace and go to heaven.

Enclose from all living-things,
How can you open fame of flag?
All that gives, ere lost in life's slave,
No fame no slander y bring from me.
Pshaw, you rouse from all happiness,
In the midst of a throng-fair what I get.

From mountain to hillock I run I run,
Fall on the knee I cry to free the flaws.
The deadness of feelings arose on me,
In my whole life leads a bond-man,
Where you create a torment-soul for me,
Have no paths no talks my heart is torpid.
You give me a chapel to take my swear,
And I prepare my soul stroll to heaven,
Singing of hymns, "God y are the creature"
My free-soul moves where no sins have.

12. Silent night

A real story happens in a person's real life. His son whom age is 4 years and nick name is BLADEWELL, study in ENGLAND. Suddenly he is missing, not found. Years come and go but a father's excitements of coming across his beloved son soon evaporated. Some days later his father tends to forgive his son's all activities. One day it so happens his father MORKISS, out of his sense, go to a grave where what he saw, create a panic on his heart. His son isn't there but his son's name BLADEWELL posted on a round-wood in one's grave. Thus his father may think it real and frequently visited to that grave and sit down on the dust of the grave.

What the hell I feel,
In the deepest darkness
A panic on my heart!
I round the deepest forest.
An owl makes its deep cry
What the battle comes I fear
Roots of trees stretch the long
A venom snake on my steps,
Rearing sounds from the foxes
The day after the full moon day
Another queer sounds face to me
Aloneness longs the heart beats.

Now night, the midst night
I stand and I stand…..
What the horror it happens
Oh, I utter the name of God.

O' look, a vampire standing there
Its face as ugly as half burnt
The wine of blood it needs
But I need to live I need to live.
That silent night needs a 'memory'
Oh, my son, my dear son….
You are on that dismal grave
You always feel sloth at night.
You come at me oh' son
Your absence makes me yammer,
It sounds your funny roles at home
Oh, son I cry all night……
Way is long but life is short
All walk till the end of life.
In your life's short way,
Tell me the value of love.

13. The Night tour

Cheerful moments come in life when you go on a tour with your friends or family members. This poem is about a real story. The poet and his 5 friends make a journey to a certain place at night. Their planning to go on a tour is a sudden decision and within a second they prepare the journey what they need they take else. The line "they seem as hot under cold heart nearly" means the night is almost cold and his friends are in a joyful events. Another line "there also friends open mouths throbbing" means they only talk to each, they loud with a high pitch, they also dance with excitements so on. They feel a meaningful life that never found before. They think they are the king and say what it may be done, do it well. Moreover the time to reach their destination is over. So the created excitements slowly decrease from time to time. This poem i.e. repeated 'THEY' indicates indirectly that the poet is in silent mood from beginning to last and thinks what they feel in jumping all are bare earthly happiness.

When all visibilities turn in our heart
We all make the sudden comic remarks
By our hands only take some we need,
Let's go the direction where we know.

Some free gasps given by hear and there
There also friends open mouths throbbing
They make their life meaningful at all
They seem as hot under cold heart nearly.

I think they all are the showers in summer
They stretch their minds to a land of fantasy
Their hands flow hither and thither stormily
They only say' what it may be done' do well.

I think they all are in bare earthly happiness,
When the destination have a second way
All excitements they create soon evaporate
And last night seems way of joyful events.

14. In thorny ways

In thorny ways means the ways are full of thorns that you feel difficulty to walk along your path. The poem shows the path beginning from one's birth to death. From birth you are supported to live, to walk, to learn so on. All they sacrifice for you what they have. They give some ideas, sensible thoughts, sagacious advice as well as teach how to fight against wrong doers. They bless you to be a great man in future. They also teach how to find a peace bird in the blue sky. They also call the Almighty for your longest leading life. But time is never waiting for anybody. There the rules of time are happening automatically. The line "lonely all ways they leave, make a sudden break in life" means they may slander to you or they may want not to keep social relationship with you or they die somehow. So now the poet (You) lead an alones life without hopes and deeds and he wants to walk millions path but he cannot. Without dear and near the poet's life is more complicated and sorrowful. The poet's heart is torpid.

But the poet thinks something difference that without fulfilling the destination he walks, from his half way journey he is bound to free from the duties they teach. The line " From the prison I leap" means what they warn you to do the responsibilities in future is like a prison but the poet wants free from it.

When I was born
Fell down on the earth
To see the mosquito-net
I feel it my home
Someone is near me,
I think it my help-mate.

All create hundred names for me!
For rays of their future eyes,
My future may be bright....
All give me a boon of ages,
All endearments made me to walk.

All things all things they cast
A magic spell upon me so that
In thorny ways, no fear
In the darkness of sky,
My face has some hopes
I get a smile when
Some sorrows I meet.
For the peaceful blue sky,
I pick a bird from them,
All things all things they cast,
A magic spell upon me
In my childhood days I learn.

In time's unclean way,
All charioteers cozen me,
Lonely all ways they leave,
Make a sudden break in life.
I feel a devils of ill-will
Furls to my lithe-heart
It needs a millions path
but sakes not to walk.
Without hopes and deeds,
And an empty soul I bring,
A long distance from paths,
From the prison I leap.

15. Night breaks!

This poem is a happening of action with sorrowful mood. When the poet goes on his bed, he could not but express his own talks near the window. He thinks a lot and remembers a lot about the past happening events. He is standing near the window and looking at aimlessly sky that all his thoughts stretch from his mind to a dark infinite sky. The line "twinkling stars look out of hurdles" says that with the running of time the darkness falls more and the more darkness approaches the more glitters the stars look. The darkness means the hurdles or the problems in this poem. The poet says that in spite of more darkness i.e. hurdles, the stars are looking clearly in other hand the poet's eyes fill up with tears but like the night stars he cannot. He remembers the painful events already gone. Then he is walking on the floor. He also thinks that his body may turn rust with the painful events he faces so that some mosquito bites on his fuel body. At last the poet is walking near the old wood chair and sitting down with his head in vertical. For some times the poet deeply sleeps. After few minutes has he slept, than the night breaks. When from the window it is beginning to blow a cold air, the poet opens his eyes and looks the open grass land out of the window.

When all days I retire on my couch
Near the window of my tears eyes
From my thoughts to an aimlessly sky
I dream old memories begin to and fro.
When I behold out of the window
It seems as darkness falls more
Twinkling stars look out of hurdles
My eyes with old-tears never stop.
Some mosquito bites on my fuel-body
Give worries to me when I take a sleep,
When all of painful things arose on me
A wood chair on its dust cover I return.

I hear smooth sounds when night breaks
As a frequent visitors of nights they return
Whenever I open my eyes sitting on a chair
From the window a cold air begins to blow.

16. A mimic!

Can you ever hear people's cry? People do and create always moments of cries. They give different types of opinions as well as wrong decisions to anyone else. Like the mimicry, they also change their colorful attitudes in behavior. The poet expresses this type of people similar to the portiere, the kink and their talks similar to a mimic. Mimic means always change yourself what the condition occurs around you. In another words, poet describes people's talks in different moods as a mimic. The poem starts with: near the cremator where the poet arrives. The poet have to know that an unknown person have already passed away so that the nearby people are uttering about the reasons of death. Some of them say that such a good person is no more a heart-broken news. Another says it is for the God's vision. They also express his good and bad works. But the poet cannot hear anything from the person who already dies. The poet hear wants to say that life is a span of thread with full of successes or failures. In another words, people are creating wrong mimic about your success as well as your failure. What you do, they gabble. What you think, they crab. So be careful to that person who has such type of crab-mentality. Their life already become meaningless but you don't make your life useless hearing such type of mimic.

Near the cremator, I hear
Some masks utter not it well,
Other replies it is for god's vision,
But who dies never fend a bit else.
In sooth, life is transient....
A curse or a blessing leads
your all successes or failures
create the wrongs mimic-cry.
They gabble about your ill-will,
They crab your mettlesome hints,
They need a muzzy in y' r battle field,
Always they cry... they cry… they cry.
I think they are like the portiere,
They are the kink, hooking legs.
Their destination as a horde,
They make their life meaningless.